WORDSWORTH CLASSICS
OF WORLD LITERATURE

General Editor: Tom Griffith MA, MPhil

TAO TE CHING

Lao Tzu

Tao te ching

❖

Translated with Notes by Arthur Waley
With an Introduction by Robert Wilkinson

WORDSWORTH CLASSICS
OF WORLD LITERATURE

The paper in this book is produced from pure wood
pulp, without the use of chlorine or any other substance
harmful to the environment. The energy used in its
production consists almost entirely of hydroelectricity
and heat generated from waste material, thereby
conserving fossil fuels and contributing little
to the greenhouse effect.

This edition published 1997 by Wordsworth Editions Limited
Cumberland House, Crib Street, Ware, Hertfordshire SG12 9ET

ISBN 1 85326 471 7

© Wordsworth Editions Limited 1997

Wordsworth® is a registered trade mark of
Wordsworth Editions Ltd

Typeset in Great Britain by Antony Gray
Printed and bound in Denmark by Nørhaven

PREFATORY NOTE

Two systems for the romanisation of Chinese are currently in use in the West, one of Western origin – The Wade-Giles system – and the other, more recent and introduced by the Chinese themselves, called *pinyin*. Some currently available translations of and commentaries on Lao Tzu use one system and some the other, making cross-reference occasionally confusing for non-specialists. To offset this difficulty, the following convention is observed in the Introduction: the translation printed in this book uses the Wade-Giles system, and therefore key Chinese terms are given in that romanisation. At their first occurrence, however, the *pinyin* equivalent is given in square brackets immediately after the Wade-Giles version. For example, the name of the great Chinese historian of the first century BC is given as Ssu-ma Ch'ien [Sima Qian] and his work as *Shih Chi* [*Shiji*] (*Historical Records*). In about one third of cases, the two systems give the same romanization, and therefore in these instances one form only appears at the first occurrence of the word concerned.

INTRODUCTION

The *Tao te ching* [*Dao de jing*] (*The Book of The Way and its Power*) is the earliest of the classic texts of the school of Chinese thought known as Taoism (pronounced 'Daoism'). Of all Chinese classics, it is the one most frequently translated into English, with around forty versions having been made so far. The Chinese text is composed of just over five thousand characters, yet within this brief compass is summarised a view of the nature and origin of all things, and the consequences of that view in the spheres of morality and politics. The ideas put forward in this text constitute the first statement of one of the three key philosophies on which the Chinese tradition of thought rests, the other two being Confucianism and Buddhism. It is impossible to understand Chinese civilisation without a knowledge of Taoism, but even historical importance on this scale does not exhaust the significance of this text. The terse and profound utterances which make up this work do no less than articulate a perspective on the human condition which has so far proved permanent: the central ideas have yet to become dated.

Until fairly recently, authorship of the *Tao te ching* was ascribed to a single Taoist sage, Lao Tzu [Laozi] whose biography is to be found in the pages of the greatest single work of Chinese history, the *Shih chi* [*Shiji*] of Ssu-ma Ch'ien [Sima Qian], dating from the beginning of the first century BC. In Ssu-ma's text, Lao Tzu emerges as an older contemporary of Confucius (551–479 BC), a native of Li Village in the State of Ch'u [Chu], and is said to have been historian in charge of the archives of Chou [Zhou]. Confucius is said to have gone to Chou to be instructed in the rites by Lao Tzu, who bade him be rid of his arrogance, ingratiating manners and excessive ambitions. Finally disenchanted by the decline of Chou, Lao Tzu resolved to depart. When he reached the Pass, its keeper requested him to write a book on the Tao before retiring from the world, and the work we now call the *Tao te ching* was the result. Lao Tzu then departed, making his exit from history riding on a blue water-buffalo. No one knows, Ssu-ma concludes, what became of Lao Tzu thereafter.

Modern scholarship has cast doubt on almost the whole of this tradition, and the view mostly widely accepted now is that this text dates from the latter part of the aptly named Warring States period of Chinese history (480–222 BC), and that it is probably an anthology of Taoist sayings, rather than the work of one man. (Certainly, many if not all of the eighty-one chapters read as if they are composed of sub-chapters assembled by an editor.) This view rests partly on detailed arguments concerning the conventions of authorship at this time in Chinese history, but also on one very powerful and straightforward fact. That is that there is no mention of the *Tao te ching* in the text of Mencius (fourth century BC), the second great Confucian philosopher. Mencius made a point of arguing against schools of thought with which he disagreed, and he would certainly have disagreed with the Taoism of this text. All the indications are that this work was assembled in the late fourth or early third century BC. The title *Tao te ching* was given to it only in Han times (206 BC–AD 220); initially, the text was known simply as the *Lao Tzu* (which means 'old man').

The term 'Tao' is very widely used in ancient Chinese philosophical texts. Its literal meaning is 'way' or 'path', and it is a short step from this to its use to mean 'way of doing something' and hence to mean 'principle' or 'set of principles'. It is in this last sense that it is used in the *Analects* of Confucius: to follow the Way in Confucian terms is to follow the set of moral principles expounded in that text, and there are obvious analogies with the use of the term 'Way' in Christian thought. It is important to be clear, however, that in Taoism the term 'Tao' is used to mean all this and, crucially, more. The fundamental assertion of Taoist philosophy is that there is an ultimate reality, prior to both heaven and earth, and this is referred to as the Tao:

> 'There was something formless yet complete,
> That existed before heaven and earth;
> Without sound, without substance,
> Dependent on nothing, unchanging . . .
> Its true name we do not know;
> 'Way' [Tao] is the by-name that we give it.' (Chapter 25)

To understand the full implications of this assertion, it is necessary to spend some time spelling out what it means to assert that there is something that is real, ultimate and in some way the basis of all there is.

To begin with, the world of ordinary experience has as its most pronounced characteristic that it is a world of individuals subject to incessant change: nothing in it endures forever, and individuals within it, both living and inanimate, can be readily observed to come into being, pass through various intermediate states, and then pass out of existence. Further, these individuals owe their existence to the causal interactions of other individuals (using the term in a very broad sense, to include the forces at work in the universe as well as to individual entities): in other words, their existence is dependent on the existence of other things. Now it has seemed to many philosophers, firstly that there must be an ultimate reality in order to give rise to the world we experience, and secondly that this reality must not be subject to the limitations of any of the individual entities within it: how could what was merely another individual, however powerful, account for the existence of all there is? Whatever is ultimate must be radically different in nature from everything else there is, and the way in which the Tao is referred to in the *Tao te ching* makes it clear that the Taoists were fully aware of this line of thought.

Most importantly, it cannot be said that the Tao is in any meaningful sense an *individual* entity at all. To be an individual is to exist in space and time, to have a determinate period of existence, to stand in relations to other individuals, and to be describable in terms of concepts – indeed, the very function of concepts is precisely to pick out, in the universe, individuals and their properties. None of these things is true of the Tao. Instead of the term 'concept' the *Tao te ching* uses the term 'name' and the memorable opening words of the first chapter make it clear that no concepts whatever apply to the Tao:

> The Way [Tao] that can be told of is not an Unvarying Way;
> The names that can be named are not unvarying names.
> It was from the Nameless that Heaven and Earth sprang.

The Nameless is that to which in principle no names (i.e. concepts) apply because it is not an individual. Anything 'that can be told of' (i.e. can be described in concepts) is not (and indeed logically cannot be) the 'Unvarying Way', the changeless, everlasting ultimate reality that is the Tao. Further, it is this basic property of being unconceptualisable that leads the Taoists to refer to the Tao in terms of the image of the Uncarved Block (Chapters 15, 19, 28, 32 and 57): like the Tao, the Uncarved Block is formless yet has within it the potential for all forms (Chapter 21) and 'Once the block is carved, there will be names' (Chapter 32) i.e. concepts apply only when individuals have arisen from the Tao. It follows from these assertions that, strictly speaking, nothing can be said about the Tao at all: it is beyond all conceptual description, and so is _ineffable_. Strictly speaking again, it follows that the words of the *Tao te ching* are attempts to say what cannot be said. Its writers were perfectly aware of this, and this awareness lies behind hesitant turns of phrase such as 'Were I forced to say to what class of things it belongs I would call it Great' (Chapter 25): the text includes a set of hints designed to push us towards the ultimate insight into reality enjoyed by the Sages – we will return to the question of the nature of this insight presently.

To repeat, even though, strictly speaking, nothing can be said about the Tao, some hints have to be given about its nature, or else those without insight could never be set on the path to a grasp of it. The only way to do this is to describe it in largely negative terms, suggesting indefiniteness in all respects, since such a description is the least misleading there can be. Hence the Tao is described, for example, as Not-being rather than Being (Chapter 40). Much as is the case with the concept of the Void to be found in certain forms of Indian philosophy, 'Not-being' is used here to mean not absolute nothingness, but rather that which is wholly indefinite, having no definable properties in contrast to Being, which is the mode of existence of definable individuals. (It is to be stressed that there is no parallel in Chinese thought to the Christian belief that a God created the universe *ex nihilo,* from sheer nothingness.) Again, the Tao is described as elusive, rarefied and infinitesimal (Chapter 14), and

> Its rising brings no light;
> Its sinking, no darkness.
> Endless the series of things without name
> On the way back to where there is nothing
> > > [i.e. Not-being]. (Chapter 14)

It is also described as lowly (Chapter 34), as like a valley (Chapters 6 and 28); like a female (Chapters 6, 10 and 28) and as being like water (Chapters 8 and 78), and all these images are meant to indicate passivity, receptivity and indefiniteness, and, in the case of the female, generativity also: the Tao is, in this sense, the mother of all things. (Chapter 52).

The image of the Tao as female leads naturally to the question of cosmogony: how did the Tao give rise to the universe? There is no detailed answer to this question in the *Tao te ching*. The nearest there is to an answer comes in Chapter 42: 'Tao gave birth to the One; the One gave birth successively to two things, three things, up to ten thousand.' (The number ten thousand is not to be taken literally: the phrase 'the ten thousand things' or 'creatures' is a standard locution in works of this period for 'all there is' or 'the entire universe' e.g. Chapter 34). This passage becomes more intelligible if compared to a parallel statement in the second masterpiece of Taoist philosophy, the *Chuang Tzu* [*Zhuangzi*], (*The book of) Master Chuang* (third century BC): 'In the great beginning, there was non-being. It had neither being nor name. The One originates from it, it has oneness but not yet physical form. When things obtain it and come into existence, that is called virtue (which gives them their individual character).' (*Chuang Tzu,* Chapter 12, Chan Wing-tsit's version). The One, then, is that which has Being but no form: the best analogue in Western terms is that of Chaos, being but without order or definiteness. From the One or Chaos arise individuals, i.e. the 'two' entities with identifiable, discriminable forms, and so on up to the richness and multiplicity of the universe as we know it. (The extremely difficult logical question of quite how not-Being can give rise to Being, in Western terms the problem of the One and the Many, is not addressed in the *Tao te ching:* the text is in philosophical terms a summary of conclusions. The arguments on which they are based must be sought elsewhere.)

The passage from the *Chuang Tzu* book refers to 'virtue' which gives to things 'their individual character'. The Chinese term translated as 'virtue' is *te* [*de*], the other term in the Han title for our present text. The word is rendered by Waley in this translation as 'power'. The discrepancy between this version and that of Professor Chan just quoted is more apparent than real: as is usually the case in versions of ancient Chinese texts, differences of this kind indicate a conceptual non-alignment between that language and modern English. There is no single concept in modern English which covers quite what the ancient Chinese concept of *te* covers. 'Virtue', not in

the moral sense as the opposite of vice, but in the value-neutral sense
of 'specific property', captures part of what is meant, and 'power'
does justice to the idea of latent force also present in the concept *te*.
Te is that in virtue of which a thing is what it is, conceived of as a
nature which has a certain force or driving power, and which
individual things receive from the Tao (cf. Chapter 51). Despite the
fact that *te* occurs in the Han title for the present text, it does not have
the degree of importance in it which this prominence might at first
sight suggest.

So far, we have been concerned with the metaphysics of Taoism as
presented in the *Tao te ching*. Before moving on to look at the other
main themes of the work, namely the implications of this outlook in
the moral and political spheres, it is as well to sum up these abstract
and unobvious ideas: the bedrock metaphysical assertion is that
behind the constantly changing everyday world of 'the ten thousand
things' (i.e. all there is) there lies an ultimate and everlasting reality,
the Tao. Strictly speaking, the Tao is ineffable. It is that which is prior
to all individuation (the Nameless) and to which no conceptual
descriptions apply. Its nature can only be hinted at by largely negative
terms such as 'not being' 'elusive' 'rarefied' and the like. It gives rise
to the world of Being, i.e. of individuals, and can be described
metaphorically as their mother. Each individual thing in the universe
has a nature *te*, which it receives from the Tao.

The easiest way to see how these ideas might affect the way we
conduct ourselves in the world is via the concept of action. An
action, as distinct from a mere event, is a change initiated by an agent,
an agent being an individual who has the property of self-conscious-
ness. (Let us leave out of account the complex issue of whether
certain animals can be regarded as either self-conscious or agents.) In
order for there to be actions at all, then, there must be self-conscious
individuals in a world which permits of modification. Further, actions
are manifestations of purposes. We have motives, desires, wishes and
so on which direct our actions, manifesting themselves as our
purposes, and purposes are properties of individual selves. Now, as
we have seen, the Tao is not an individual of any kind and is not
within the realm of the changeable; therefore the Tao cannot be said,
even metaphorically, to act. Hence is arrived at a further key doctrine
of Taoism, namely that the way of the Tao is *wu-wei*, non-action: it
'acts without action, does without doing' (Chapter 63), or again:

> Tao never does;
> Yet through it all things are done.
>
> (Chapter 37)

Because the Tao is not an individual, it logically cannot be said to act; yet, because it is the mother of all there is, whatever is done is done ultimately because of the Tao. The way in which the Tao gives rise to the universe cannot be described as an action: the nearest metaphorical description which can be given is the notion of pure spontaneity. Occasionally, we cry or jump for joy and so on in a way which surprises even ourselves: the ego which has purposes is as much astonished as the rest of the world when such things occur, and to call such events actions at all is to stretch the concept, since they are not manifestations of purposes. The Tao, of course, is not an ego; to say that whatever it brings about is done utterly spontaneously is merely the least misleading way there is, in a language designed to articulate how human beings act, of describing how the Tao brings things about. (Those familiar with the Vedanta school of Hindu thought will be aware of a reasonable analogue in that philosophy. The ultimate reality in Vedanta is Brahman, which is described much as is the Tao. When asked: why does Brahman manifest itself as a universe at all, the best answer that can be given is *lila,* the Sanskrit term for sport or play, by which is meant sheer spontaneity.)

The next major assertion in the Taoist outlook is this: human beings may so conduct themselves as to be in accord with the Tao, or they may not. The individual who lives in accord with the Tao is the Sage, *sheng* or *sheng jen* [*sheng ren*]. Since the way of the Tao is *wu-wei,* that is what the Sage must seek to emulate: hence, as is stated in a number of places in the *Tao te ching,* 'the Sage relies on actionless activity' (Chapter 2; cf. Chapter 43 or Chapter 27). Since the whole of the moral and political philosophy of the *Tao te ching* rests on this assertion, it is necessary at this point to spend some time working out what it means to do this. What must a Taoist Sage be like, and what precisely is it like to carry out 'actionless activity'?

As we have seen, the way of the Tao is *wu-wei* because the Tao is not an individual. Therefore, if the Sage is to accomplish the attainment of *wu-wei,* then he (or she) must become as much like the Tao, and therefore as little like an individual, as possible: this is what is meant by 'returning' to the Tao (Chapter 25; cf. Chapter 40). The actions of individuals involve purposes, and purposes are the result of the desires and wishes of the ego. Accordingly, the fewer the desires and wishes of the ego, the closer we come to the Tao, and the less individual we become. Hence, the Sage does not strive for any personal end (Chapter 7); diminishes personal desire to the greatest possible degree and so knows 'the contentment that comes simply through being content' (Chapter 46); day by day subtracts from knowledge (since knowledge of things stimulates desire for them) and so arrives at 'inactivity' (Chapter 48). The Sage speaks very little, for words embody conceptual distinctions and so lead us further from the Tao (Chapters 17, 23 and 56); desires nothing and so has a mind which simply, like a mirror, reflects impartially and desirelessly what is before it – such a one appears to the world like a child or an idiot (Chapters 10, 20 and 49). The further the Sage progresses along the path of diminishing the force and role of the ego, the closer his approach to the Tao. Whatever the Sage does will not be the result of selfish desires, since these desires have been eliminated. Accordingly, whatever the Sage does will not be 'action' in a proper sense at all, but *wu-wei*, activity which is not action, a purely spontaneous manifestation of the Tao.

When the ego has been thoroughly subdued, the Sage arrives at the mystical experience which lies at the root of Taoism, an experience referred to in the *Tao te ching* as illumination, *ming* (Chapters 16, 33 and 55). This is direct acquaintance with reality, the Tao. Ordinarily, when we are in the condition in which our life is directed to the satisfaction of our desires, we are more or less constantly unquiet: no sooner is one desire satisfied than another arises, and then another, and so on, relentlessly. The Sage, by subduing or perhaps even destroying the ego, breaks this sequence, and arrives at a condition of inner peace or quietness of an intensity which the non-illumined cannot even guess at. Hence:

> Quietness is called submission to Fate;
> What has submitted to Fate has become part of the always-so.
> To know the always-so is to be illumined;
> Not to know it, means to go blindly to disaster. (Chapter 16)

The Sage has no personal desires, and so submits unprotestingly to the course of events (Fate); those in this condition know the Tao ('the always-so') and they know it by illumination. Elsewhere, Waley translates *ming* as the 'inner light' (e.g. Chapter 52) and this indicates an important point about mystical experience: the reality which is encountered is found *within* us, not outside us. The journey to the Tao is a journey inwards. Ordinarily, the Tao is hidden or obscured by the ego and its desires: once these are dissipated, the Tao can be experienced. The Tao is like a wireless signal buried in static: once reception clears, i.e. once the ego is put in <u>abeyance</u>, the signal appears. The analogy cannot be pushed too far, however: there is a distinction between the clear signal and the person listening to it; whereas, in mystical experience, there is no meaningful distinction to be made between the Tao and the Sage.

The text of the *Tao te ching* does not tell us by means of what disciplines or techniques the ego is to be subdued, and for the answer one must look to other Taoist works. In common with other philosophical systems based on a mystical experience, like advaita Vedanta or Zen, what is involved is a long and testing set of yogic practices designed to dissipate the ego. This is why we are exhorted to 'Block the passages, shut the doors' (Chapter 52), i.e. cut ourselves off from outer stimuli by means of meditational techniques. (For a short and accessible account of Taoist yoga, see the work by Odier listed in the bibliography.) Nor does the *Tao te ching* give us a description of what it is like to be a Sage, to engage in actionless activity. The reason is largely that it is a condition almost impossible to describe in language which has evolved precisely to describe ordinary purposive action. Yet some mystics do try to give us a clue as to what it is like. One such was the Japanese Zen master Bankei (AD 1622–93). Bankei's word for the ultimate reality is the Unborn (in Japanese *fusho*) and those who are illumined (have experienced what in Zen is called *satori*), like the Taoist Sages, manifest pure spontaneity. Bankei describes to an acquaintance who was a devotee of the martial arts what it would be like to fight after *satori*: 'When, without thinking and without acting deliberately, you manifest the Unborn, you won't have any fixed form. When you are without fixed form, no opponent will exist for you in the whole land. Not holding on to anything, not relying one-sidedly on anything, there is no 'you' and no 'enemy'. Whatever comes you just respond, with no traces left behind.' (Bankei: *Instructions to Layman Gesso* in Peter Haskel [ed and tr]: *Bankei Zen*, Grove Weidenfeld, New York 1984, pp. 138–9). The Sage has no ego and so does not deliberate. What the Sage does is to respond with *absolute* spontaneity to the conditions in the world.

All the ideas considered so far form the basis of the moral and political views set out in the *Tao te ching*. The state of Chinese society at the time these ideas were formulated was such as to make these issues matters of the most urgent concern. At the time of the Warring States, China as a unified country did not exist, and as this description suggests, consisted of a set of smaller states unceasingly engaged in wars of conquest against one another. Human life in such times of constantly threatening chaos and death is not to be envied, and all the philosophies developed at the time included suggestions as to how this condition of chronic instability might be overcome. For the Taoist, not unexpectedly, such a condition is interpreted as the result of a serious departure from the way of the Tao, and therefore what the Sage seeks to do, both as private citizen and as ruler, is to return people as closely as possible to conformity with the Tao, and this principle underlies all the moral and political recommendations of the *Tao te ching*.

In the moral sphere, the Sage seeks to diminish the knowledge and the desires of the people: as has been seen, these concepts are intimately linked, since it is knowledge of things which usually causes us to desire them: hence: 'In the days of old those who practised Tao with success did not, by means of it, enlighten the people, but on the contrary sought to make them ignorant.' (Chapter 65; cf. Chapter 19). The less people desire, the less they will be unquiet and unhappy: not everyone can attain sagehood, but all can be made less greedy and less envious than they are. Further, the Sage regards the cultivation of morality in the form of virtues or rules – in the Confucian manner, for example – as evidence of serious failure to be in accord with the Tao. This is the thought behind the remark,

> It was when the Great Way declined
> That human kindness and morality arose.
>
>   (Chapter 18; cf. Chapter 38)

Human kindness or benevolence, *jen* [*ren*], is the key virtue in Confucianism. The Taoist criticism of Confucianism is that the latter deals only with symptoms, as it were, and does not go to the heart of the matter. The whole Confucian apparatus of cultivation of virtue and observance of the rites operates at the level of the surface ego. Confucianism does not include the concept of the Tao as ultimate reality, nor the possibility of direct acquaintance with it when the surface ego disintegrates after yogic training. Confucianism therefore embodies complete ignorance of the most significant truths about the universe.

Closely related to these points is the distinction between learning and wisdom:

> True wisdom is different from much learning;
> Much learning means little wisdom. (Chapter 81)

This is because learning is concerned with the everyday world and how it works: the more one becomes absorbed in studies of this kind, the more one becomes involved in fineness of conceptual discrimination and the more remote, therefore, one becomes from the divisionless way of the Tao. The Sage, of course, has wisdom and this is why, to repeat a point mentioned above, he appears dull and speaks little. Anyone who is glib or fluent, the Taoist would say, can be assumed with certainty to be no Sage, but merely caught in the web of conceptual discriminations which conceals reality.

The political disorder of the time the Taoists saw as what happens when the desires of the surface ego are reinforced by access to political power: greed, envy, lust for glory and the wish for one ego to triumph over another generate war and all the evils that come with it. The path to peace and to the Taoist vision of utopia lies in simplifying society to the greatest possible extent: rid society of institutions and structures which promote greed, envy and artificial desires (i.e. desires for goods or statuses which it would not have occurred to anyone to want had not some scheming politician invented them) and the people will more closely approach true contentment, i.e. not the state in which desires are satisfied, but the state in which the desires to be satisfied have been diminished to the greatest possible degree. This is the belief behind such recommendations as these:

> The more prohibitions there are, the more ritual avoidances,
> The poorer the people will be . . .
> The more cunning craftsmen there are,
> The more pernicious contrivances will be invented.
> The more laws are promulgated,
> The more thieves and bandits there will be.
>
> (Chapter 57 and 3)

The Sage rules,

> By emptying their hearts
> And filling their bellies,
> Weakening their intelligence
> And toughening their sinews,
> Ever striving to make the people
>   knowledgeless and desireless.

(Chapter 3)

Unenlightened rulers are those at the mercy of the desires of the ego. They are unquiet, unable to leave things alone, constantly formulating new goals, new plans, all (from the Taoist point of view) valueless and artificial. Constant political activity is an index and result of departure from the Tao, and will surely end in disaster (Chapters 26 and 29). The Sage, by contrast, does as little as possible (Chapters 37, 59, 60 and 61). Left to themselves in a state of simplicity, the people are easy to handle (Chapter 75). Best of all for them is to live in a Taoist utopia, a small and simple community without hierarchies or any of the artifices of so-called civilisation. In such a community, the people would be truly content just to have enough to eat, to be simply clad and to be occupied with rustic work. They would live and die without travelling anywhere, and would be entirely happy to do so (Chapter 80; cf. *Chuang Tzu,* Chapter 10). They would have nothing to desire, and so would be at peace; and this is to be close to the Tao. War is the result of desire (Chapters 30 and 31): destroy the desire, and you banish war.

Such in outline is the Taoist philosophy of the *Tao te ching,* but before concluding this brief survey two important points remain to be made. The first is that the philosophical Taoism discussed here should not be confused with the Taoist religion which developed in the second century AD. Chinese historians distinguish the two, the philosophical school being *tao chia* [*dao jia*], and the religion *tao chiao* [*dao jiao*]. The religion of Taoism produced an enormous body of scripture and related texts, the Tao Tsang [Dao zang] or Taoist Canon numbering some 1,464 titles. A great deal of attention is devoted in this religion to the quest for immortality, and the search for an alchemical elixir was pursued with great vigour.

Secondly, it would be difficult to overstress the role Taoist philosophy has played in Chinese spiritual, artistic and intellectual life. In the description of the Tao given above, in order to furnish a clear line of exposition the emphasis was placed on the strictly philosophical properties of the Tao – its ineffability, divisionlessness and so on. Yet it would be quite misleading not to make clear that the Tao was at the same time conceived far less abstractly. Taoists do not make a radical distinction between the Tao and the order of Nature in general; or, put another way, would regard the Tao as in some sense present in or informing all there is: indeed, if all things receive their *te* from the Tao, then in an important sense the Tao must be present in all things. Thus for the Taoist, Nature is (as we would say) divine, and once Nature is regarded as divine it becomes at once an object of reverence and worthy of the most careful attention. This belief lies behind a good deal of Chinese aesthetics and also stimulated the scientific study of the natural order: see the works by Chang and Needham in the bibliography below, for detailed discussions of these consequences of Taoism.

Philosophical ideas do not last so long or affect so many aspects of life unless they are of considerable profundity. Works which we call profound have, among other properties, the ability to touch some deep and abiding chord in human nature, and further to stimulate creativity and insightful reflection apparently without end. The terse and often beautiful statements of the *Tao te ching* do both these things to this day. The view of the universe and of how we should respond to it summarised in this short book remains one of the major options open to us.

ROBERT WILKINSON
Senior Lecturer in Philosophy
The Open University in Scotland

SUGGESTIONS FOR FURTHER READING

Other major Taoist works

Burton Watson (tr), *The Complete Works of Chuang Tzu*, Columbia
    University Press, New York 1970

A. C. Graham (tr), *The Book of Lieh-Tzu*, Mandala, London 1991

There are also very useful selections from the *Tao te ching, Chuang
    Tzu* and *Lieh-tzu* in:

Chan Wing-tsit (ed & tr): *A Source Book in Chinese Philosophy*,
    Princeton University Press, New Jersey 1963

Introductory works on Taoism

M. Kaltenmark and Roger Greaves (tr), *Lao Tzu and Taoism,*
    Stanford University Press, California 1969

A. Watts, *Tao: The Watercourse Way*, Penguin, Harmondsworth 1979

More advanced works dealing with various aspects of Taoism

Chang Chung-yuan: *Creativity and Taoism,* Wildwood House,
    London 1975

Fung Yu-lan and Derk Bodde (tr), *A History of Chinese Philosophy,*
    Princeton University Press, New Jersey, Volume I (2nd edition)
    1952, Volume II 1953

J. Needham, *Science and Civilisation in China,* Volume II, Cambridge
    University Press, England 1956

D. Odier and John Mahoney (tr), *Nirvana Tao: The Secret Meditation
    Techniques of the Taoist and Buddhist Masters,* East West
    Publications, London and the Hague 1986

NOTE ON THE TEXT

The text printed here is the translation by Arthur Waley, without his
paraphrases and commentaries. The footnotes are also Waley's. They
are reprinted as in the 1968 edition, except that those dealing with
points of purely philological interest have been deleted.

Chapter 1

The Way that can be told of is not an Unvarying Way:

The names that can be named are not unvarying names.

It was from the Nameless that Heaven and Earth
    sprang;

The named is but the mother that rears the ten
    thousand creatures, each after its kind.

Truly, 'Only he that rids himself forever of desire can
    see the Secret Essences';

He that has never rid himself of desire can see only the
    Outcomes.

These two things issued from the same mould, but
    nevertheless are different in name.

This 'same mould' we can but call the Mystery,

Or rather the 'Darker than any Mystery',

The Doorway whence issued all Secret Essences.

Chapter 2

It is because every one under Heaven recognizes beauty
    as beauty, that the idea of ugliness exists.

And equally if every one recognized virtue as virtue,
    this would merely create fresh conceptions of
    wickedness.

For truly 'Being and Not-being grow out of one
    another;

Difficult and easy complete one another.

Long and short test one another;

High and low determine one another.

Pitch and mode give harmony to one another.

Front and back give sequence to one another'.

Therefore [1] the Sage relies on actionless activity,

Carries on wordless teaching,

But the myriad creatures are worked upon by him; he
    does not disown them.

He rears them, but does not lay claim to them,

Controls them, but does not lean upon them,

Achieves his aim, but does not call attention [2] to what
    he does;

And for the very reason that he does not call attention
    to what he does

He is not ejected from fruition of what he has done.

---

1 Because 'action' can only make one thing high at the expense of making
  something else low, etc.
2 literally, 'does not place (i.e. classify) himself as a victor'. cf. Mencius II, I;
  2.

Chapter 3

If we stop looking for 'persons of superior morality' *(hsien)* to put in power, there will be no more jealousies among the people. If we cease to set store by products that are hard to get, there will be no more thieves. If the people never see such things as excite desire, their hearts will remain placid and undisturbed. Therefore the Sage rules

> By emptying their hearts
> And filling their bellies,
> Weakening their intelligence[1]
> And toughening their sinews
> Ever striving to make the people knowledgeless
>   and desireless.

Indeed he sees to it that if there be any who have knowledge, they dare not interfere. Yet through his actionless activity all things are duly regulated.

---

1 Particularly in the sense of 'having ideas of one's own'.

Chapter 4

The Way is like an empty vessel
That yet may be drawn from
Without ever needing to be filled.
It is bottomless; the very progenitor of all things in
    the world.
In it all sharpness is blunted,
All tangles untied,
All glare tempered,
All dust[1] smoothed.
It is like a deep pool that never dries.
Was it too the child of something else? We cannot
    tell.
But as a substanceless image[2] it existed before the
    Ancestor.[3]

1 Dust is the Taoist symbol for the noise and fuss of everyday life.
2 A *hsiang*, an image such as the mental images that float before us when
   we think.
3 The Ancestor in question is almost certainly the Yellow Ancestor who
   separated Earth from Heaven and so destroyed the Primal Unity, for
   which he is frequently censured in *Chuang Tzu*.

Chapter 5

Heaven and Earth are ruthless;
To them the Ten Thousand Things are but as
    straw dogs.
The Sage too is ruthless;
To him the people are but as straw dogs.
Yet [1] Heaven and Earth and all that lies between
Is like a bellows
In that it is empty, but gives a supply that never
    fails.
Work it, and more comes out.
Whereas the force of words [2] is soon spent.
Far better is it to keep what is in the heart. [3]

1 Though ruthless nature is perpetually bounteous.
2 Laws and proclamations.
3 For *chung* as 'what is within the heart', see *Tso Chuan*, Yin Kung 3rd year
   and *Kuan Tzu*, 37, beginning. The comparison of Heaven and Earth to a
   bellows is also found in *Kuan Tzu* (P'ien 11, beginning).

Chapter 6

The Valley Spirit never dies.
It is named the Mysterious Female.
And the Doorway of the Mysterious Female
Is the base from which Heaven and Earth sprang.
It is there within us all the while;
Draw upon it as you will, it never runs dry.[1]

---

1 *Lieh Tzu* quotes these lines as coming from the *Book of the Yellow Ancestor;* but it does not follow that the *Tao Ching* is actually quoting them from this source. They may belong to the general stock of early Taoist rhymed teaching. For *ch'in* compare below, Chapter 52, line 9, and *Huai-nan Tzu* I, fol. 2.

Chapter 7

Heaven is eternal, the Earth everlasting.
How come they to be so? Is it because they do not
    foster their own lives;
That is why they live so long.
Therefore the Sage
Puts himself in the background; but is always to
    the fore.
Remains outside; but is always there.
Is it not just because he does not strive for any
    personal end
That all his personal ends are fulfilled?

Chapter 8

The highest good is like that of water. The goodness of water is that it benefits the ten thousand creatures; yet itself does not scramble, but is content with the places that all men disdain. It is this that makes water so near to the Way.

And if men think the ground the best place for building
    a house upon,
If among thoughts they value those that are profound,
If in friendship they value gentleness,
In words, truth; in government, good order;
In deeds, effectiveness; in actions, timeliness –
In each case it is because they prefer what does not lead
    to strife,[1]
And therefore does not go amiss.

1 Even ordinary people realize the importance of the Taoist principle of 'water-like' behaviour, i.e. not striving to get on top or to the fore.

Chapter 9

Stretch a bow[1] to the very full,
And you will wish you had stopped in time;
Temper a sword-edge to its very sharpest,
And you will find it soon grows dull.
When bronze and jade fill your hall
It can no longer be guarded.
Wealth and place breed insolence
That brings ruin in its train.
When your work is done, then withdraw!
Such is Heaven's[2] Way.

1 The expression used can also apply to filling a vessel to the brim; but
   'stretching a bow' makes a better parallel to 'sharpening a sword'.
2 as opposed to the Way of man.

Chapter 10

Can you keep the unquiet physical-soul from straying,
  hold fast to the Unity, and never quit it?

Can you, when concentrating your breath, make it soft
  like that of a little child?

Can you wipe and cleanse your vision of the Mystery
  till all is without blur?

Can you love the people and rule the land, yet remain
  unknown?

Can you in opening and shutting the heavenly gates
  play always the female part?

Can your mind penetrate every corner of the land, but
  you yourself never interfere?

Rear them, then, feed them,

Rear them, but do not lay claim to them.

Control them, but never lean upon them;

Be chief among them, but do not manage them.

This is called the Mysterious Power.

Chapter 11

We put thirty spokes together and call it a wheel;
But it is on the space where there is nothing that
    the usefulness of the wheel depends.
We turn clay to make a vessel;
But it is on the space where there is nothing that
    the usefulness of the vessel depends.
We pierce doors and windows to make a house;
And it is on these spaces where there is nothing
    that the usefulness of the house depends.
Therefore just as we take advantage of what is, we
    should recognise the usefulness of what is not.

Chapter 12

The five colours confuse the eye,
The five sounds dull the ear,
The five tastes spoil the palate.
Excess of hunting and chasing
Makes minds go mad.
Products that are hard to get
Impede their owner's movements.
Therefore the Sage
Considers the belly not the eye.[1]
Truly, 'he rejects that but takes this'.[2]

---

1 The belly in this instance means 'what is inside him', his own inner powers.
2 For this use of 'that' and 'this' (i.e. the world outside and the powers within oneself) cf. *Kuan Tzu*, 36, middle.

Chapter 13

'Favour and disgrace goad as it were to madness;[1] high rank hurts keenly as our bodies hurt.' What does it mean to say that favour and disgrace goad as it were to madness? It means that when a ruler's subjects[2] get it[3] they turn distraught, when they lose it they turn distraught. That is what is meant by saying favour and disgrace goad as it were to madness. What does it mean to say that high rank hurts keenly as our bodies hurt? The only reason that we suffer hurt is that we have bodies; if we had no bodies, how could we suffer? Therefore we may accept the saying: 'He who in dealing with the empire regards his high rank as though it were his body is the best person to be entrusted with rule; he who in dealing with the empire loves his subjects as one should love one's body is the best person to whom one can commit the empire.'

1 see additional notes.
2 *Hsia.*
3 i.e. favour.

Chapter 14

Because the eye gazes but can catch no glimpse of it,
It is called elusive.
Because the ear listens but cannot hear it,[1]
It is called the rarefied.
Because the hand feels for it but cannot find it,
It is called the infinitesimal.
These three because they cannot be further
    scrutinized,
Blend into one.
Its rising brings no light;
Its sinking, no darkness.
Endless the series of things without name
On the way back to where there is nothing.
They are called shapeless shapes;
Forms without form;
Are called vague semblances.
Go towards them, and you can see no front;
Go after them and you see no rear.
Yet by seizing on the Way that was
You can ride[2] the things that are now.
For to know what once there was,[3] in the
    Beginning,
This is called the essence[4] of the Way.

1 This is the traditional description of ghosts and spirits (cf. *Doctrine of the Mean*, paragraph 16) adopted as a description of the Way.
2 i.e. dominate.
3 Macrocosmically, in the Universe. Microcosmically, in oneself.
4 literally, main-thread.

Chapter 15

Of old those that were the best officers of Court

Had inner natures subtle, abstruse, mysterious,
    penetrating,

Too deep to be understood.

And because such men could not be understood

I can but tell of them as they appeared to the
    world:

Circumspect they seemed, like one who in winter
    crosses a stream,

Watchful, as one who must meet danger on every
    side.

Ceremonious, as one who pays a visit;

Yet yielding, as ice when it begins to melt.

Blank as a piece of uncarved wood;

Yet receptive as a hollow in the hills.

Murky, as a troubled stream –

Which of you can assume such murkiness, to
    become in the end still and clear?

Which of you can make yourself inert, to become
    in the end full of life and stir?

Those who possess this Tao do not try to fill
    themselves to the brim,

And because they do not try to fill themselves to
    the brim

They are like a garment that endures all wear and
    need never be renewed (?).

Chapter 16

Push far enough towards the Void,

Hold fast enough to Quietness,

And of the ten thousand things none but can be
worked on by you.

I have beheld them, whither they go back.

See, all things howsoever they flourish

Return to the root from which they grew.

This return to the root is called Quietness;

Quietness is called submission to Fate;

What has submitted to Fate has become part of the
always-so.

To know the always-so is to be Illumined;

Not to know it, means to go blindly to disaster.

He who knows the always-so has room in him for
everything;

He who has room in him for everything is without
prejudice.

To be without prejudice is to be kingly;

To be kingly is to be of heaven;

To be of heaven is to be in Tao.

Tao is forever and he that possesses it,

Though his body ceases, is not destroyed.

Chapter 17

Of the highest[1] the people merely know that such
a one exists;

The next they draw near to and praise.

The next they shrink from, intimidated; but revile.

Truly, 'It is by not believing people that you turn
them into liars.'[2]

But from the Sage it is so hard at any price to get a
single word[3]

That when his task is accomplished, his work
done,

Throughout the country every one says 'It
happened of its own accord'.

---

1 i.e. most Taoist.
2 The same saying is quoted in Chapter 23. cf. Chapter 49: 'The truthful
man I believe; but the liar I also believe, and so he (the liar) gets
truthfulness.' Similarly it is 'lack' in the ruler which creates in the people
every other fault and crime.
3 literally: 'How, reluctant, he raises the price of his words!'

Chapter 18

It was when the Great Way declined
That human kindness and morality arose;
It was when intelligence and knowledge
    appeared
That the Great Artifice began.
It was when the six near ones [1] were no
    longer at peace
That there was talk of 'dutiful sons';[2]
Nor till fatherland was dark with strife
Did we hear of 'loyal slaves'.[3]

---

1 father, son, elder brother, younger brother, husband and wife.
2 read *tzu* 'son' not *tz'u* 'compassionate', as in the *Yung Lo Ta Tien* text.
3 as Ministers called themselves.

Chapter 19

Banish wisdom, discard knowledge,
And the people will be benefited a hundredfold.
Banish human kindness, discard morality,
And the people will be dutiful and compassionate.
Banish skill, discard profit,[1]
And thieves and robbers will disappear.
If when these three things are done[2] they find life
    too plain and unadorned,
Then let them have accessories;
Give them Simplicity to look at, the Uncarved
    Block to hold,
Give them selflessness and fewness of desires.

---

1 i.e. do away with skilful artisans and enterprising traders, who supply
things likely to attract thieves.
2 I suspect that a negative has fallen out in front of 'these three', and that
the original ran: 'If without these three . . . they find life, etc.'

Chapter 20

Banish learning,[1] and there will be no more
    grieving.

Between *wei* and *o*

What after all is the difference?

Can it be compared to the difference between
    good and bad? [2]

The saying 'what others avoid I too must avoid'

How false and superficial it is!

All men, indeed, are wreathed in smiles,

As though feasting after the Great Sacrifice,

As though going up to the Spring Carnival.[3]

I alone am inert, like a child that has not yet given
    sign;[4]

Like an infant that has not yet smiled.

I droop and drift, as though I belonged nowhere.

All men have enough and to spare;

I alone seem to have lost everything.

1 'Learning' means in particular learning the '3300 rules of etiquette'. *Wei*
  and *o* were the formal and informal words for 'yes', each appropriate to
  certain occasions. For 'learning' in the sense of knowing which words are
  taboo at which courts, see *Kuo Yü, 15,* fol. 3.
2 Good and bad in the Taoist sense, i.e. like and unlike the Way. This leads
  up to the description of the great gulf that separates the Taoist from other
  men. This description is in the form of a generalised *jung* (see Chapter 15,
  above) and cannot be taken as in any sense a self-portrait of the author.
  The sense of the first six lines is very doubtful.
3 see additional notes. I read *teng ch'un t'ai*.
4 A child 'gives sign' by stretching its hand towards some object. This is an
  important omen concerning its future.

Mine is indeed the mind of a very idiot,
So dull am I.
The world is full of people that shine;
I alone am dark.
They look lively and self assured;
I alone, depressed.
I seem unsettled[5] as the ocean;
Blown adrift, never brought to a stop.
All men can be put to some use;
I alone am intractable and boorish.
But wherein I most am different from men
Is that I prize no sustenance that comes not from
    the Mother's[6] breast.

5 for this sense of *tan*, see *Lü Shih Ch'un Ch'iu, P'ien* 111, line 7.
6 i.e. the Way's. The image may equally well be that of a child in the
   womb, 'feeding on the mother'.

Chapter 21

Such the scope of the All-pervading Power
That it alone can act through the Way.
For the Way is a thing impalpable,
    incommensurable.
Incommensurable, impalpable.
Yet latent in it are forms;[1]
Impalpable, incommensurable
Yet within it are entities.
Shadowy it is and dim;
Yet within it there is a force,
A force that though rarefied
Is none the less efficacious.
From the time of old till now
Its charge[2] has not departed
But cheers onward the many warriors.
How do I know that the many warriors are so?
Through this.[3]

1 thought–images, ideas.
2 see additional notes.
3 through inward knowledge, intuition.

Chapter 22

'To remain whole, be twisted!'
To become straight, let yourself be bent.
To become full, be hollow.
Be tattered, that you may be renewed.
Those that have little, may get more,
Those that have much, are but perplexed.
Therefore the Sage
Clasps the Primal Unity,
Testing by it everything under heaven.
He does not show himself; therefore he is seen
    everywhere.
He does not define himself, therefore he is distinct.
He does not boast of what he will do, therefore he
    succeeds.
He is not proud of his work, and therefore it
    endures.
He does not contend,
And for that very reason no one under heaven can
    contend with him.
So then we see that the ancient saying 'To remain
    whole, be twisted!' was no idle word; for true
    wholeness can only be achieved by return.[1]

1 to the Way.

Chapter 23

To be always talking is against nature. For the same reason a hurricane never lasts a whole morning, nor a rainstorm all day. Who is it that makes the wind and rain? It is Heaven-and-Earth.[1] And if even Heaven-and-Earth cannot blow or pour for long, how much less in his utterance should man? Truly, if one uses the Way[2] as one's instrument, the results will be like the Way; if one uses the 'power' as one's instrument, the results will be like the power. If one uses what is the reverse of the 'power', the results will be the reverse of the 'power'. For to those who have conformed themselves to the Way, the Way readily lends its power. To those who have conformed themselves to the power, the power readily lends more power. While to those who conform themselves to inefficacy, inefficacy readily lends its ineffectiveness. 'It is by not believing in people that you turn them into liars.'[3]

---

1 'Nature', as we should say.
2 The text is here somewhat confused; but the general meaning is clear.
3 see above, Chapter 17. If one uses disbelief as one's instrument of government, the result will be a nation of liars.

Chapter 24

'He who stands on tip-toe, does not stand firm;
He who takes the longest strides, does not walk the
 fastest.'
He who does his own looking sees little,
He who defines himself is not therefore distinct.
He who boasts of what he will do succeeds in
 nothing;
He who is proud of his work, achieves nothing
 that endures.
Of these, from the standpoint of the Way, it is said:
'Pass round superfluous dishes to those that have
 already had enough,
And no creature but will reject them in disgust.'
That is why he that possesses Tao does not linger.[1]

1 over the scene of his successes, thus calling attention to them.
 cf. Chapter 2.

Chapter 25

There was something formless yet complete,
That existed before heaven and earth;
Without sound, without substance,
Dependent on nothing, unchanging,
All pervading, unfailing.
One may think of it as the mother of all things
    under heaven.
Its true name [1] we do not know;
'Way' is the by-name that we give it.
Were I forced to say to what class of things it
    belongs I should call it Great *(ta)*.
Now *ta* also means passing on,
And passing on means going Far Away,
And going far away means returning. [2]

Thus just as Tao [3] has 'this greatness' and as earth has it and as heaven has it, so may the ruler also have it. Thus 'within the realm there are four portions of greatness', and one belongs to the king. The ways of men are conditioned by those of earth. The ways of earth, by those of heaven. The ways of heaven by those of Tao, and the ways of Tao by the Self-so. [4]

1 i.e. we do not know to what class of things it belongs.
2 returning to 'what was there in the Beginning'.
3 Henceforward I shall use the Chinese word Tao instead of the Way; to
   do so avoids many inconveniences.
4 the 'unconditioned'; the 'what-is-so-of-itself'.

Chapter 26

As the heavy must be the foundation of the light,

So quietness is lord and master of activity.

Truly, 'A man of consequence[1] though he travels
all day

Will not let himself be separated from his baggage-
wagon,[2]

However magnificent the view, he sits quiet and
dispassionate'.

How much less, then, must the lord of ten
thousand chariots

Allow himself to be lighter[3] than these he rules!

If he is light, the foundation is lost;

If he is active, the lord and master[4] is lost.

1 reading *Chün-tzu*, which has considerable ancient support; cf. Ma Hsü-
lun's *Lao Tzu Fu Ku*.
2 literally, 'his covered heavy', 'heavy' being the Chinese name for carts as
opposed to light travelling carriages. There is a play on the two senses of
'heavy'. This is a patrician proverb, a maxim of the *chün-tzu*, 'gentlemen'.
3 i.e. more easily moved.
4 i.e. quietness, the magical passivity that is also called *wu-wei*. There is a
secondary meaning: 'His lordship is lost'.

Chapter 27

Perfect activity leaves no track behind it;
Perfect speech is like a jade-worker whose tool leaves
    no mark.
The perfect reckoner needs no counting-slips;[1]
The perfect door has neither bolt nor bar,
Yet cannot be opened.
The perfect knot needs neither rope nor twine,
Yet cannot be untied.
Therefore the Sage
Is all the time in the most perfect way helping men,
He certainly does not turn his back on men;
Is all the time in the most perfect way helping creatures,
He certainly does not turn his back on creatures.
This is called resorting to the Light.[2]
Truly, 'the perfect man is the teacher of the imperfect;
But the imperfect is the stock-in-trade[3] of the perfect
    man'.
He who does not respect his teacher,
He who does not take care of his stock-in-trade,
Much learning though he may possess, is far astray.
This[4] is the essential secret.

1 slips of bamboo thrown into little bowls; forerunner of the abacus.
2 'Light' has been defined above as self-knowledge. 'This' means the way
  in which the Sage saves the world, though apparently shunning it.
3 cf. *Chuang Tzu*, I, 4.
4 The power to influence mankind through Tao. The commonest charge
  brought against Taoists was that of being merely interested in self-
  perfection without regard for the welfare of the community as a whole.
  The present chapter is devoted to rebutting that charge.

Chapter 28

'He who knows the male, yet cleaves to what is female
Becomes like a ravine, receiving all things under
    heaven,'[1]
And being such a ravine
He knows all the time a power that he never calls upon
    in vain.
This is returning to the state of infancy.
He who knows the white, yet cleaves to the black
Becomes the standard by which all things are tested;
And being such a standard
He has all the time a power that never errs,
He returns to the Limitless.
He who knows glory, yet cleaves to ignominy
Becomes like a valley that receives into it all things
    under heaven,
And being such a valley
He has all the time a power that suffices;
He returns to the state of the Uncarved Block.
Now when a block is sawed up it is made into
    implements;[2]
But when the Sage uses it, it becomes Chief of all
    Ministers.
Truly, 'The greatest carver[3] does the least cutting'.

---

1 adapted from a Lao Tan saying. See *Chuang Tzu*, XXXIII, 5.
2 play on the double sense of this word which also means 'a subordinate',
    'an instrument of government'.
3 play on *chih* 'to cut', 'to carve', and *chih* 'to rule'. The secondary meaning
    is that the greatest ruler does the least chopping about.

Chapter 29

Those that would gain what is under heaven[1] by tampering with it – I have seen that they do not succeed. For that which is under heaven is like a holy vessel, dangerous to tamper with.

Those that tamper with it, harm it.

Those that grab at it, lose it.

For among the creatures of the world some go in front, some follow;

Some blow hot when others would be blowing cold.

Some are feeling vigorous just when others are worn out.

Some are loading just when others would be tilting out.

Therefore the Sage 'discards the absolute, the all-inclusive,[2] the extreme'.

1 i.e. empire.
2 *Shê* means (1) spread out (2) dissipated. It is the first meaning which is appropriate here The author is however certainly adapting a maxim that was aimed against dissipation, luxury etc. cf. *Han Fei Tzu*, P'ien 8, beginning.

Chapter 30

He who by Tao purposes to help a ruler of men
Will oppose all conquest by force of arms;
For such things are wont to rebound.[1]
Where armies are, thorns and brambles grow.
The raising of a great host
Is followed by a year of dearth.[2]
Therefore a good general effects his purpose and then stops;
    he does not take further advantage of his victory.
Fulfils his purpose and does not glory in what he has done;
Fulfils his purpose and does not boast of what he has done;
Fulfils his purpose, but takes no pride in what he has done;
Fulfils his purpose, but only as a step that could not be
    avoided.[3]
Fulfils his purpose, but without violence;
For what has a time of vigour also has a time of decay.
This[4] is against Tao,
And what is against Tao will soon perish.

1 literally: 'To be reversed'. He who overcomes by violence will himself be
  overcome by violence.
2 This does not only refer to direct destruction, but also to the curse that
  war brings upon herds and crops by its intrinsic 'balefulness'.
3 For the construction compare *Chuang Tzu* XXIII, 6: 'To move only
  when movement cannot be avoided, that is the true power.' This
  principle of *pu tê i*, 'action as a last resort' was preached by the 4th
  century Quietist Shên Tao, and pervades *Chuang Tzu*.
4 violence.

Chapter 31

Fine[1] weapons are none the less ill-omened things. That is why, among people of good birth,[2] in peace the left-hand side[3] is the place of honour, but in war this is reversed and the right-hand side is the place of honour. The Quietist,[4] even when he conquers, does not regard weapons as lovely things. For to think them lovely means to delight in them, and to delight in them means to delight in the slaughter of men. And he who delights in the slaughter of men will never get what he looks for out of those that dwell under heaven. A host that has slain men is received with grief and mourning; he that has conquered in battle is[5] received with rites of mourning.

---

1 *Chia* also means 'auspicious', e.g. *chia jih,* 'a lucky day'. I see no reason to tamper with the text.
2 of good birth, and consequently of good manners.
3 see additional notes.
4 for this expression cf. *Han Fei Tzu,* P'ien 51, near end and *Chuang Tzu* X, end.
5 Whether such a custom actually existed we do not know; but we learn from *Huai-nan Tzu* (15, end) that the general, having received his marching orders, cuts his nails (as was done by mourners before a funeral), dresses in mourning garb and leaves the city by a 'gate of ill-omen' constructed for the purpose.

Chapter 32

Tao is eternal, but has no fame (name);

The Uncarved Block,[1] though seemingly of small
    account,

Is greater than anything that is under heaven.[2]

If kings and barons would but possess themselves
    of it,

The ten thousand creatures would flock to do
    them homage;

Heaven-and-earth would conspire

To send Sweet Dew,[3]

Without law or compulsion, men would dwell in
    harmony.

Once the block is carved,[4] there will be names,[5]

And so soon as there are names

Know that it is time to stop.

Only by knowing when it is time to stop can
    danger be avoided.

To Tao[6] all under heaven will come

As streams and torrents flow into a great river or
    sea.

1 see Chapter 28.
2 literally: 'under Heaven no one dares regard it as an inferior.'
3 'Sweet Dew tastes like barley-sugar or honey; it falls only when a
   kingdom is at complete peace.' *Lun Hêng* XIX, 2. See also *Kuan Tzu*,
   P'ien 20, fol. 16 and *Lü Shih Ch'un Ch'iu* 115, end.
4 secondary meaning 'Once there is government'.
5 categories, distinctions. Things depending on contrast with something
   else; as opposed to Tao which 'is so of itself'.
6 i.e. to the possessor of Tao. The last two lines resume the thought of lines
   4 and 5.

Chapter 33

To understand others is to have knowledge;
To understand oneself is to be illumined.
To conquer others needs strength;
To conquer oneself is harder still.
To be content with what one has is to be rich.
He that works through [1] violence may get his way;
But only what stays [2] in its place
Can endure.
When one dies one is not lost; [3] there is no other
    longevity.

---

1 the word *hsing* implies movement as well as action.
2 as, for example, mountains.
3 One's left arm may become a cock; one's right arm a bow; one's buttocks wheels (*Chuang Tzu* VI, 6). In any case, no part of one will be lost.

Chapter 34

Great Tao is like a boat that drifts;
It can go this way; it can go that.
The ten thousand creatures owe their existence to
    it and it does not disown them;
Yet having produced them, it does not take
    possession of them.[1]
Tao, though it covers the ten thousand things like
    a garment,
Makes no claim to be master over them,
And asks for nothing from them.
Therefore it may be called the Lowly:
The ten thousand creatures obey it,
Though they know not that they have a master;
Therefore it is called the Great.
So too the Sage just because he never at any time
    makes a show of greatness in fact achieves
    greatness.

1 cf. Chapter 2 where similar words are used of the Sage, who is identified
   with Tao.

Chapter 35

He who holding the Great Form goes about his
    work in the empire
Can go about his work, yet do no harm.
All is peace, quietness and security.
Sound of music, smell of good dishes
Will make the passing stranger pause.
How different the words that Tao gives forth!
So thin, so flavourless!
If one looks for Tao, there is nothing solid to see;
If one listens for it, there is nothing loud enough to
    hear.
Yet if one uses it, it is inexhaustible.

Chapter 36

What is in the end to be shrunk
Must first be stretched.
Whatever is to be weakened
Must begin by being made strong.
What is to be overthrown
Must begin by being set up.
He who would be a taker
Must begin as a giver.
This is called 'dimming' one's light.[1]
It is thus that the soft overcomes the hard
And the weak, the strong.
'It is best to leave the fish down in his pool;
Best to leave the State's sharpest weapons
    where none can see them.'

---

1 *Wei* means (1) 'obscure because so small', (2) 'obscure because so dark'. It
   is etymologically connected with *mei* 'dark'.

Chapter 37

Tao never does;
Yet through it all things are done.
If the barons and kings would but possess
    themselves of it,
The ten thousand creatures would at once be
    transformed.
And if having been transformed they should desire
    to act
We must restrain them by the blankness[1] of the
    Unnamed.
The blankness of the Unnamed
Brings dispassion;
To be dispassionate is to be still,
And so,[2] of itself, the whole empire will be at rest.

1 literally, 'the uncarven-wood-quality'.
2 if the Sage is 'still'.

Chapter 38

The man of highest 'power' does not reveal himself as a
   possessor of 'power';

Therefore he keeps his 'power'.

The man of inferior 'power' cannot rid it of the appearance of
   'power';

Therefore he is in truth without 'power'.

The man of highest 'power' neither acts[1] nor is there any who
   so regards him;[2]

The man of inferior 'power' both acts and is so regarded.[3]

The man of highest humanity, though he acts, is not so
   regarded;

Whereas a man of even the highest morality both acts and is so
   regarded.

While even he who is best versed in ritual not merely acts, but
   if people fail to respond

Then he will pull up his sleeves and advance upon them.

That is why it is said:[4] 'After Tao was lost, then came the
   "power";

After the "power" was lost, then came human kindness.

After human kindness was lost, then came morality.

After morality was lost, then came ritual.

Now ritual is the mere husk[5] of loyalty and promise-keeping

---

1 Does not act separately and particularly but only applies the power in a
   general way.
2 Regards him as a possessor of power. Compare *Kuan Tzu*, P'ien 5,
   paragraph 2.
3 i.e. is regarded as a possessor of *tê*.
4 the same saying is quoted by *Chuang Tzu*, XXII, 1.
5 or 'attenuated form'; but it balances *hua* ('flower', as opposed to fruit) and
   it is better to indicate the vegetable metaphor.

And is indeed the first step towards brawling.'
Foreknowledge[6] may be the 'flower of doctrine',
But it is the beginning of folly.
Therefore the full-grown man[7] takes his stand upon the solid
    substance and not upon the mere husk,
Upon the fruit and not upon the flower.
Truly, 'he rejects that and takes this'.

6 see additional notes.
7 'full-grown' in Tao.

Chapter 39

As for the things that from of old have understood the
    Whole –
The sky through such understanding remains limpid,
Earth remains steady,
The spirits keep their holiness,[1]
The abyss is replenished,
The ten thousand creatures bear their kind,
Barons and princes direct their people.
It is the Whole that causes it.
Were it not so limpid, the sky would soon get torn.
Were it not for its steadiness, the earth would soon tip
    over.
Were it not for their holiness, the spirits would soon
    wither away.
Were it not for this replenishment, the abyss would
    soon go dry.
Were it not that the ten thousand creatures can bear
    their kind,
They would soon become extinct.
Were the barons and princes no longer directors of their
    people and for that reason honoured and exalted,
    they would soon be overthrown.
Truly 'the humble is the stem upon which the mighty
    grows,
The low is the foundation upon which the high is laid.'

---

1 Their *ling*, which is to spirits (or objects and animals 'possessed' by spirits)
  what *tê* is to man. It is cognate to words meaning life, name, command,
  etc.

That is why barons and princes refer to themselves as
'The Orphan', 'The Needy', 'The Ill-provided'. Is
this not indeed a case of might rooting itself upon
humility?

True indeed are the sayings:
'Enumerate the parts of a carriage, and you still have not explained
what a carriage is', and 'They[2] did not want themselves to tinkle like
jade-bells, while others resounded like stone-chimes.'

2 the Sages of old

Chapter 40

In Tao the only motion is returning;[1]
The only useful quality, weakness.
For though all creatures under heaven are the
     products of Being,
Being itself is the product of Not-being.

1 cf. Chapter 25, line 12.

Chapter 41

When the man of highest capacities hears Tao
He does his best to put it into practice.
When the man of middling capacity hears Tao
He is in two minds about it.
When the man of low capacity hears Tao
He laughs loudly at it.
If he did not laugh, it would not be worth the name of Tao.
Therefore the proverb has it:
'The way[1] out into the light often looks dark,
The way that goes ahead often looks as if it went back.'
The way that is least hilly often looks as if it went up
    and down,
The 'power' that is really loftiest looks like an abyss,
What is sheerest white looks blurred.
The 'power' that is most sufficing looks inadequate,
The 'power' that stands firmest looks flimsy.
What is in its natural, pure state looks faded;
The largest square has no corners,
The greatest vessel takes the longest to finish,[2]
Great music has the faintest[3] notes,
The Great Form[4] is without shape.
For Tao is hidden and nameless.
Yet Tao alone supports[5] all things and brings them to
    fulfilment.

1 Tao.
2 Metaphorical meaning, 'The greatest capacities develop latest'.
3 'most rarefied.' cf. Chapter 14.
4 cf. Chapter 35.
5 a commercial metaphor. Literally 'backs financially'.

Chapter 42

Tao gave birth to the One; the One gave birth successively to two things, three things, up to ten thousand.[1] These ten thousand creatures cannot turn their backs to the shade without having the sun on their bellies,[2] and it is on this blending of the breaths[3] that their harmony[4] depends. To be orphaned, needy, ill-provided is what men most hate; yet princes and dukes style themselves so. Truly, 'things are often increased by seeking to diminish them and diminished by seeking to increase them.' The maxims that others use in their teaching I too will use in mine. Show me a man of violence that came to a good end, and I will take him for my teacher.

1 i.e. everything.
2 Which symbolises the fact that they are themselves a mixture of light and dark, hard and soft, water and fire, etc.
3 the warm 'breath' of the sun and the cold 'breath' of the shade. Hence 'breath' comes to mean a 'state of the atmosphere' in a wider sense.
4 or 'balance', as we should say.

Chapter 43

What is of all things most yielding[1]

Can overwhelm that which is of all things
    most hard.[2]

Being substanceless it can enter even where
    there is no space;

That is how I know the value of action that is
    actionless.

But that there can be teaching without words,

Value in action that is actionless,

Few indeed can understand.

1 water.
2 rock.

Chapter 44

Fame or one's own self, which matters to one most?

One's own self or things bought, which should count most?

In the getting or the losing, which is worse?[1]

Hence he who grudges expense pays dearest in the end;

He who has hoarded most will suffer the heaviest loss.[2]

Be content with what you have and are, and no one can despoil you;

Who stops in time nothing can harm.

He is forever safe and secure.

1 i.e. which is better, to get fame and wealth but injure oneself, or to lack fame and wealth and save oneself?

2 He drives people to such exasperation that they attack him and help themselves. For *ai* in the sense 'grudge' compare *I Chou Shu* 54, 'He who is stingy about rewards and gifts is called *ai*'. The primary meaning of *ai* is 'to want to keep to oneself'. Hence the commoner meaning 'to love', which would here be out of place.

Chapter 45

What is most perfect seems to have something
    missing;
Yet its use is unimpaired.[1]
What is most full seems empty:
Yet its use will never fail.[2]
What is most straight seems crooked;
The greatest skill seems like clumsiness,
The greatest eloquence like stuttering.[3]
Movement overcomes cold;
But staying still overcomes heat.
So he[4] by his limpid calm
Puts right everything under heaven.

1 metaphor of a pot or vessel; applied to Tao.
2 it can be drawn upon indefinitely.
3 cf. Confucius *Analects* IV, 24.
4 the Sage.

Chapter 46

When there is Tao in the empire

The galloping[1] steeds are turned back to fertilize
the ground by their droppings.

When there is not Tao in the empire

War horses will be reared even on the sacred
mounds[2] below the city walls.

No lure[3] is greater than to possess what others
want,

No disaster greater than not to be content with
what one has,

No presage of evil greater than that men should be
wanting to get more.

Truly: 'He who has once known the contentment
that comes simply through being content, will
never again be otherwise than contented'.

---

1 i.e. carriage-horses, used not for war but for travelling. Every one will be
contented where he is.

2 see additional notes. They are reared, of course, as a preparation for
offensive war, i.e. for 'getting more'.

3 i.e. incitement to evil doers. See additional notes.

Chapter 47

Without leaving his door
He knows everything under heaven.
Without looking out of his window
He knows all the ways of heaven.
For the further one travels[1]
The less one knows.
Therefore the Sage arrives without going,
Sees all[2] without looking,
Does nothing, yet achieves everything.

1 away from Tao; away from the Unity into the Multiplicity.
2 read *ming* 'illumined', not *ming* 'name'. The two characters are constantly interchanged in old texts.

Chapter 48

Learning consists in adding to one's stock day
    by day;
The practice of Tao consists in 'subtracting
    day by day,
Subtracting and yet again subtracting
Till one has reached inactivity.
But by this very inactivity
Everything can be activated.'[1]
Those who of old won the adherence of all
    who live under heaven
All did so by not interfering.
Had they interfered,
They would never have won this adherence.

1 cf. *Chuang Tzu* XXII, 1.

Chapter 49

The Sage has no heart[1] of his own;
He uses the heart of the people as his heart.
Of the good man I[2] approve,
But of the bad I also approve,
And thus he gets goodness.
The truthful man I believe, but the liar I also
    believe,
And thus he gets truthfulness.[3]
The Sage, in his dealings with the world,
    seems like one dazed with fright;
For the world's sake he dulls his wits.
The Hundred families all the time strain their
    eyes and ears,
The Sage all the time sees and hears no more
    than an infant sees and hears.

1 ,makes no judgments of his own.
2 i.e. the Sage.
3 cf. Chapter 17 and 23.

Chapter 50

He who aims at life achieves death. If the 'companions of life'[1] are thirteen, so likewise are the 'companions of death' thirteen. How is it that the 'death-spots'[2] in man's life and activity are also thirteen? It is because men feed life too grossly. It is said that he who has a true hold on life, when he walks on land[3] does not meet tigers or wild buffaloes; in battle he is not touched by weapons of war. Indeed, a buffalo that attacked him would find nothing for its horns to butt, a tiger would find nothing for its claws to tear, a weapon would find no place for its point to enter in.[4] And why? Because such men have no 'death-spot' in them.

1 The four limbs and nine apertures that constitute the human apparatus.
2 a military expression.
3 One would expect this to balance a clause about what happens when he is on the water.
4 cf. *Chuang Tzu*, XVII, 1, end.

Chapter 51

Tao gave them birth;
The 'power' of Tao reared them,
Shaped them according to their kinds,
Perfected them, giving to each its strength.[1]

Therefore of the ten thousand things[2] there is not one that does not worship Tao and do homage to its 'power'. No mandate ever went forth that accorded to Tao the right to be worshipped, nor to its 'power' the right to receive homage.

It was always and of itself so.

Therefore as Tao bore them and the 'power' of Tao reared them, made them grow, fostered them, harboured them, brewed[3] for them, so you[4] must

'Rear them, but not lay claim to them,
Control them, but never lean upon them,
Be chief among them, but not manage them.
This is called the mysterious power.'[5]

---

1 Its 'strong point', inborn capacity.
2 excepting Man?
3 The word means a 'decoction', whether nutritive, medicinal or (as always in modern Chinese) poisonous.
4 the Sage.
5 cf. Chapter 10.

Chapter 52

That which was the beginning of all things under
    heaven
We may speak of as the 'mother' of all things.
He who apprehends the mother [1]
Thereby knows the sons.[2]
And he who has known the sons
Will hold all the tighter to the mother,
And to the end of his days suffer no harm:
'Block the passages, shut the doors,
And till the end your strength shall not fail.
Open up the passages, increase your doings,
And till your last day no help shall come to you.'
As good sight means seeing what is very small
So strength means holding on to what is weak.[3]
He who having used the outer-light [4] can return to
    the inner-light
Is thereby preserved from all harm.
This is called resorting to the always-so.

1 Tao, the One, the Whole.
2 the Many, the universe.
3 i.e. Tao.
4 this corresponds to 'knowing the sons'. *Ming* ('inner light') is self-
    knowledge.

Chapter 53

He who has the least scrap[1] of sense, once he has got
started on the great highway has nothing to fear so long as
he avoids turnings. For great highways are safe and easy.

> But men love by-paths.[2]
> So long as the Court is in order
> They are content to let their fields run to weed
> And their granaries stand empty.
> They wear patterns and embroideries,
> Carry sharp swords, glut themselves with drink and
>   food, have more possessions than they can use.
> These are the riotous ways of brigandage;[3] they are
>   not the Highway.

1 see additional notes.
2 All this is of course metaphorical. The highway is Tao; the bypaths, the
   Confucian virtues. 'Loving by-paths' implies also neglecting the essential
   and pursuing the secondary.
3 compare the riotous ways of the Robber Chê in *Chuang Tzu*.

Chapter 54

What Tao[1] plants cannot be plucked,

What Tao clasps, cannot slip.

By its virtue alone can one generation after another carry on
    the ancestral sacrifice. [2]

Apply it to yourself and by its power you will be freed from dross.

Apply it to your household and your household shall thereby
    have abundance.

Apply it to the village, and the village will be made secure.

Apply it to the kingdom, and the kingdom shall thereby be
    made to flourish.

Apply it to an empire, and the empire shall thereby be extended.

Therefore just as through[3] oneself one may contemplate Oneself,

So through the household one may contemplate the Household,[4]

And through the village, one may contemplate the Village,

And through the kingdom, one may contemplate the Kingdom,

And through the empire, one may contemplate the Empire.

How do I know that the empire is so?

By this.[5]

---

1 literally 'what is well planted', i.e. planted by Tao.
2 The 'power' of the ancestor's Tao carries the family on.
3 By delving back through the successive stages of one's own consciousness
   one gets back to the Unity of the Whole which is one's Tao. cf. the *Maitri
   Upanishad* 'having seen the Self through oneself one becomes selfless'.
4 i.e the Tao of the household. When one has had vision of the Tao
   (underlying essence) of a thing, one can control it. This catena (self-
   household–village, etc) is found in every branch of Chinese philosophy,
   applied in a variety of ways. It originated I think with the Yang Chu
   theory that to perfect a family one must perfect the individual members
   of it, to perfect a village one must perfect each several family, etc.
5 what is inside me.

Chapter 55

The impunity of things fraught with the 'power'

May be likened to that of an infant.

Poisonous insects do not sting it,

Nor fierce beasts seize it,

Nor clawing birds maul it.

Its bones are soft, its sinews weak: but its grip is strong.

Not yet to have known the union of male and female,
    but to be completely formed,

Means that the vital force is at its height;

To be able to scream all day without getting hoarse

Means that harmony[1] is at its perfection.

To understand such harmony[2] is to understand the
    always-so.

To understand the always-so is to be illumined.

But to fill life to the brim is to invite omens.[3]

If the heart makes calls upon the life-breath,[4] rigidity
    follows.

Whatever has a time of vigour also has a time of decay.

Such[5] things are against Tao,

And whatever is against Tao is soon destroyed.

---

1 of hot and cold, soft and hard, etc.

2 cf. *Analects*, I, 12.

3 Here, as in the Short Preface to the *Book of History* and *Shih Chi*,
  Chapter III, fol. 6, *hsiang* means a bad omen. It originally meant a portent
  of any kind, whether good or bad. In current Chinese it is, of course,
  only used in the favourable sense.

4 The emotions were thought by the Chinese to make call upon and use
  up the original supply of breath which was allotted to a man at birth and
  constituted his life-spirit.

5 filling to the brim, calling upon the life-breath, having a time of 'vigour'.
  cf. Chapter 30.

Chapter 56

Those who know do not speak;
Those who speak do not know.
Block the passages,
Shut the doors,
Let all sharpness be blunted,
All tangles untied,
All glare tempered.
All dust smoothed.[1]
This is called the mysterious levelling.[2]
He who has achieved it cannot either be drawn
    into friendship or repelled,
Cannot be benefited, cannot be harmed,
Cannot either be raised or humbled,
And for that very reason is highest of all creatures
    under heaven.

1 cf. Chapter 4.
2 In which there is a general perception not effected through particular
  senses. See *Lieh Tzu* II, 3. 'Henceforward my eyes were one with my
  ears, my ears with my nose, my nose with my mouth . . . '

Chapter 57

'Kingdoms can only be governed if rules are kept;
Battles can only be won if rules are broken.'[1]
But the adherence of all under heaven can only be won by
   letting-alone.
How do I know that it is so? By this.[2]
The more prohibitions there are, the more ritual avoidances,
The poorer the people will be.
The more 'sharp weapons'[3] there are,
The more benighted will the whole land grow.
The more cunning craftsmen there are,
The more pernicious contrivances[4] will be invented.
The more laws are promulgated,
The more thieves and bandits there will be.
Therefore a sage has said:
So long as I 'do nothing' the people will of themselves be
   transformed.
So long as I love quietude, the people will of themselves go
   straight.
So long as I act only by inactivity the people will of
   themselves become prosperous.
So long as I have no wants the people will of themselves
   return to the 'state of the Uncarved Block'.

---

1 A military maxim, to the pattern of which the author proceeds to fit his
   Taoist formula. *Ch'i* means unexpected manoeuvres. *Chêng* 'rules kept' is
   not here used in its technical military sense of 'open attack'.
2 see Chapter 12. Through what I have found inside myself, 'in the belly';
   through the light of my inner vision.
3 i.e. clever people.
4. cf. the story in *Chuang Tzu* (XII, II) about the man in whom the idea of
   a simple labour-saving contrivance inspired feelings similar to those
   aroused in Wordsworth by the sight of a railway train.

Chapter 58

When the ruler looks depressed[1] the people will
    be happy and satisfied;
When the ruler looks lively and self–assured[2] the
    people will be carping and discontented.
'It is upon bad fortune that good fortune leans,
    upon good fortune that bad fortune rests.'[3]
But though few know it, there is a bourn where
    there is neither right nor wrong; [4]
In a realm where every straight is doubled by a
    crooked, and every good by an ill, surely
    mankind has gone long enough astray?
Therefore the Sage
Squares without cutting,
Shapes the corners without lopping,
Straightens without stretching,
Gives forth light without shining.[5]

1 as the Taoist is described as doing in Chapter 20.
2 like the people of the world in Chapter 20.
3 Such are the maxims that pass as wisdom. The author is here manifestly
   satirizing a passage in the *Lü Shih Ch'un Ch'iu* (Pi'en 29, beginning): 'It is
   upon bad fortune that good fortune leans, upon good fortune that bad
   fortune rests. The Sage alone perceives this. How should ordinary men
   reach such a bourn (of wisdom)?' To the Taoist the real 'bourn of
   wisdom' lies far beyond the world of contraries and antinomies.
4 *Hsieh*, omitted by some versions of the Wang Pi text, should be retained.
5 Through Tao he reaches his *ends* without the use of *means*. To translate
   'shines without dazzling' is to misunderstand the whole sequence. The
   Confucians as their 'means' use the virtues of 'squareness', i.e. rectitude
   and 'angularity' i.e. incorruptibility.

Chapter 59

You cannot rule men nor serve heaven unless you have
    laid up a store;

This 'laying up a store' means quickly absorbing.

And 'quickly absorbing' means doubling one's garnered
    'power'.

Double your garnered power and it acquires a strength
    that nothing can overcome.

If there is nothing it cannot overcome, it knows no
    bounds,

And only what knows no bounds

Is huge enough to keep a whole kingdom in its grasp.

But only he who having the kingdom goes to the
    Mother

Can keep it long.

This[1] is called the art of making the roots strike deep by
    fencing the trunk, of making life long by fixed
    staring.

1 i.e. going to Tao the Mother.

Chapter 60

Ruling a large kingdom is indeed like cooking small fish.[1]
They who by Tao ruled all that is under heaven did not let
an evil spirit within them display its powers. Nay, it was not
only that the evil spirit did not display its powers, neither
was the Sage's good spirit used to the hurt of other men.
Nor was it only that his good spirit was not used to harm
other men, the Sage himself was thus saved from harm.
And so, each being saved from harm, their 'powers' could
converge towards a common end.

1 the less one handles them the better.

Chapter 61

A large kingdom must be like the low ground towards which all streams flow down. It must be a point towards which all things under heaven converge. Its part must be that of the female in its dealings with all things under heaven. The female by quiescence conquers the male; by quiescence gets underneath.[1] If a large kingdom can in the same way succeed in getting underneath a small kingdom then it will win the adherence of the small kingdom; and it is because small kingdoms are by nature in this way underneath large kingdoms that they win the adherence of large kingdoms. The one must get underneath in order to do it; the other is underneath and therefore does it. What large countries really need is more inhabitants; and what small countries need is some place where their surplus inhabitants can go and get employment. Thus[2] each gets what it needs. That is why I say the large kingdom must 'get underneath'.

---

1 literally: 'becomes underneath', i.e. induces the male to mount her.
2 i.e. if the large kingdom 'gets underneath'. It is assumed that the population of the large kingdom will be relatively sparse; that of the small kingdom relatively dense.

Chapter 62

Tao in the Universe is like the south-west corner[1] in
    the house.
It is the treasure of a good man,
The support of the bad.
There is a traffic in speakers of fine words;
Persons of grave demeanour are accepted as gifts;
Even the bad let slip no opportunity to acquire them.
Therefore[2] on the day of the Emperor's enthronement
Or at the installation of the three officers of State
Rather than send a team of four horses, preceded by a
    disc of jade,
Better were it, as can be done without moving from
    one's seat, to send this Tao.

For what did the ancients say of this Tao, how did they
prize it? Did they not say of those that have it: 'Pursuing,
they shall catch; pursued, they shall escape?' They thought
it, indeed, most precious of all things under heaven.

1 Where family worship was carried on; the pivotal point round which the
household centred.
2 i.e. if things other than presents in kind are not only accepted as gifts, but
even purchased at high price.

Chapter 63

It acts without action, does without doing, finds
    flavour in what is flavourless,[1]
Can make the small great and the few many,
'Requites injuries with good deeds,
Deals with the hard while it is still easy,
With the great while it is still small.'[2]
In the governance of empire everything difficult
    must be dealt with while it is still easy,
Everything great must be dealt with while it is still
    small.
Therefore the Sage never has to deal with the
    great; and so achieves greatness.
But again 'Light assent inspires little confidence
And "many easies" means many a hard.'
Therefore the Sage knows too how to make the
    easy difficult, and by doing so avoid all
    difficulties!

---

1 in Chapter 35 Tao itself is said to be 'flavourless'.
2 compare *Han Fei Tzu,* 38. The saying originally merely meant 'attend to
   troubles in time, before they get out of hand'.

Chapter 64

'What stays still is easy to hold;
Before there has been an omen it is easy to lay plans.
What is tender is easily torn,[1]
What is minute is easy to scatter.'
Deal with things in their state of not-yet-being,
Put them in order before they have got into confusion.
For 'the tree big as a man's embrace began as a tiny
    sprout,
The tower nine storeys high began with a heap of earth,
The journey of a thousand leagues began with what was
    under the feet'.
He who acts, harms; he who grabs, lets slip.
Therefore the Sage does not act, and so does not harm;
Does not grab, and so does not let slip.
Whereas the people of the world, at their tasks,
Constantly spoil things when within an ace of
    completing them.
'Heed the end no less than the beginning,
 And your work will not be spoiled.
Therefore[2] the Sage wants only things that are
    unwanted,
Sets no store by products difficult to get,

---

1 Reading *p'an* with the 'knife' determinative; or 'What is soft is easily
  melted', if we keep the 'water' determinative.
2 Because the 'end' (the world around us) is as important as the 'beginning'
  (the primal state, the One, the Whole). The Sage does not only work
  through Tao; he also shows the world the degree to which ordinary life
  can be moulded to the pattern of Tao.

And so teaches things untaught,

Turning all men back to the things they have left
    behind,[3]

That the ten thousand creatures may be restored to their
    Self-so[4]

This he does; but dare not act.

---

3 Such as walking instead of riding, using knotted ropes instead of writing,
   etc. See Chapter 80.

4 To what they are of themselves, as opposed to what they are in relation
   to other things.

Chapter 65

In the days of old those who practised Tao with success did not, by means of it, enlighten the people, but on the contrary sought to make them ignorant.

> The more knowledge people have, the harder they
>   are to rule.
> Those who seek to rule by giving knowledge
> Are like bandits preying on the land.
> Those who rule without giving knowledge
> Bring a stock of good fortune to the land.
> To have understood the difference between these
>   two things is to have a test and standard.
> To be always able to apply this test and standard
> Is called the mysterious 'power',
> The mysterious 'power', so deep-penetrating,
> So far-reaching,
> That can follow things back –
> All the way back to the Great Concordance.[1]

1 cf. *Chuang Tzu*, XII, 8.

Chapter 66

How did the great rivers and seas get their kingship
  over the hundred lesser streams?

Through the merit of being lower than they; that
  was how they got their kingship.

Therefore the Sage

In order to be above the people

Must speak as though he were lower than the
  people.

In order to guide them

He must put himself behind them.

Only thus can the Sage be on top and the people
  not be crushed by his weight.

Only thus can he guide, and the people not be led
  into harm.

Indeed in this way everything under heaven will be glad to
be pushed by[1] him and will not find his guidance irksome.
This he does by not striving; and because he does not
strive, none can contend with him.

1 'from behind'.

Chapter 67

Every one under heaven says that our Way is greatly like folly. But it is just because it is great, that it seems like folly. As for things that do not seem like folly[1] – well, there can be no question about *their* smallness!

Here are my three treasures.[2] Guard and keep them! The first is pity; the second, frugality; the third, refusal to be 'foremost of all things under heaven'.

> For only he that pities is truly able to be brave;
> Only he that is frugal is truly able to be profuse.
> Only he that refuses to be foremost of all things
> Is truly able to become chief of all Ministers.[3]

At present your bravery is not based on pity, nor your profusion on frugality, nor your vanguard on your rear;[4] and this is death. But pity cannot fight without conquering or guard without saving. Heaven arms with pity those whom it would not see destroyed.[5]

1 literally: 'that seem normal'.
2 The three rules that formed the practical, political side of the author's teaching (1) abstention from aggressive war and capital punishment, (2) absolute simplicity of living, (3) refusal to assert active authority.
3 The phrase has exactly the same meaning as the *kuan-ch'ang* of Chapter 28.
4 i.e. your eminence on self-effacement. This is as perilous as to leave one's line of communication undefended.
5 Such is the sense that our author gives to the saying. It is probable, however that it is simply a couplet from some old ritual-song (like those in the last part of the *Book of Odes*) and means 'Heaven deigned to help them; in its pity it protected them'.

Chapter 68

The best charioteers do not rush ahead;
The best fighters do not make displays of wrath.[1]
The greatest conqueror wins without joining issue;
✝ The best user of men acts as though he were their
    inferior.
This is called the power that comes of not
    contending,
Is called the capacity to use men,
The secret of being mated to heaven, to what was
    of old.

1 *Nu* is anger shown outwardly, as by glaring, grimacing or the like.

Chapter 69

The strategists have the sayings: 'When you doubt your
ability to meet the enemy's attack, take the offensive
yourself', and 'If you doubt your ability to advance an inch,
then retreat a foot'.

This latter is what we call to march without moving,
To roll the sleeve, but present no bare arm,
The hand that seems to hold, yet has no weapon in it,
A host that can confront, yet presents no battle-front.
Now the greatest of all calamities is to attack and find
    no enemy.
I can have no enemy only at the price of losing my
    treasure.
Therefore when armies are raised and issues joined it is
    he who does not delight in war that wins.

Chapter 70

My words are very easy to understand and very easy to put into practice. Yet no one under heaven understands them; no one puts them into practice. But my words have an ancestry, my deeds have a lord;[1] and it is precisely because men do not understand this that they are unable to understand me.

Few then understand me; but it is upon this very fact that my value depends. It is indeed in this sense[2] that 'the Sage wears hair-cloth on top, but carries jade underneath his dress'.

1 To have 'neither ancestors nor lord' was to be a wild man, a savage. This is a metaphorical way of saying that all the Sage did and said was related to a definite system of thought.
2 In this sense, and not in the sense that he flies in panic from the horrors of the world. Rich people, in times of tumult, dressed up as peasants and hid their jade treasures under their clothes. Metaphorically 'to wear haircloth' etc., came to mean 'to hide one's light under a bushel', 'to keep one's knowledge to oneself'.

Chapter 71

'To know when one does not know is best.
To think one knows when one does not know is a dire
    disease.
Only he who recognizes this disease as a disease
Can cure himself of the disease.'
The Sage's way of curing disease
Also consists in making people recognize their diseases
    as diseases and thus ceasing to be diseased.

Chapter 72

Never mind if the people are not intimidated by your authority. A Mightier Authority[1] will deal with them in the end. Do not narrow their dwellings[2] or harass their lives;[3] and for the very reason that you do not harass them, they will cease to turn from[4] you. Therefore the Sage knows himself[5] but does not show himself. Knows his own value, but does not put himself on high. Truly, 'he rejects that but takes this'.[6]

1 heaven. cf. *I Chou Shu,* P'ien 67.
2 i.e. put them in prison.
3 literally: 'that whereby they live', their livelihoods. The author is thinking of heavy taxation and the like.
4 There is a pun on 'harass' and 'turn from'. The root means originally 'to press down from above'. Hence (1) to oppress (2) to have food crammed into one, to be 'fed up', to turn away in disgust.
5 i.e. knows his own power, but does not display it.
6 see Chapter 12.

Chapter 73

He whose braveness lies in daring, slays.
He whose braveness lies in not daring,[1] gives life.
Of these two, either may be profitable or unprofitable.
But 'Heaven hates what it hates;
None can know the reason why'.[2]
Wherefore the Sage too disallows it.
For it is the way of Heaven not to strive but none the
    less to conquer,
Not to speak, but none the less to get an answer,
Not to beckon; yet things come to it of themselves.
Heaven is like one who says little, yet none the less has
    laid his plans.
Heaven's net is wide;
Coarse are the meshes, yet nothing slips through.

1 i.e. in not daring to slay.
2 Heaven hates the shedding of blood (i.e. it is 'against nature'), and those
who ignore the will of Heaven are bound to be trapped at last in the
meshes of Fate. This is the traditional pacifist argument of the Mo Tzu
school, which our author is here able to utilize by identifying Heaven
with Tao. For 'Heaven hates what it hates . . . ' cf. *Lieh Tzu* VI, 5.

Chapter 74

The people are not frightened of death. What then is the use of trying to intimidate them with the death-penalty? And even supposing people were generally frightened of death and did not regard it as an everyday thing, which of us would dare to seize them and slay them?[1] There is the Lord of Slaughter[2] always ready for this task, and to do it in his stead is like thrusting oneself into the master-carpenter's place and doing his chipping for him. Now 'he who tries to do the master-carpenter's chipping for him is lucky if he does not cut his hand'.[3]

1 i.e. even supposing the death-penalty really had the effect of scaring people and keeping down crime, is it fair to ask anyone to undertake such a task?
2 i.e. heaven or its agents (pestilence, famine, lightning, earthquake, etc.).
3 adaptation of a proverb meaning 'let every man stick to his task'.

Chapter 75

The people starve because those above them eat too much tax-grain. That is the only reason why they starve. The people are difficult to keep in order because those above them interfere. That is the only reason why they are so difficult to keep in order. The people attach no importance to death, because those above them are too grossly absorbed in the pursuit of life. That is why they[1] attach no importance to death. And indeed, in that their hearts are so little set on life they are superior to those who set store by life.[2]

---

1 the people.
2 i.e. are superior to their rulers; so that there is no chance of the state being well governed.

Chapter 76

When he is born, man is soft and weak; in death he becomes stiff and hard. The ten thousand creatures and all plants and trees while they are alive are supple and soft, but when they are dead they become brittle and dry. Truly, what is stiff and hard is a 'companion of death'; what is soft and weak is a 'companion of life.[1] Therefore 'the weapon that is too hard[2] will be broken, the tree that has the hardest wood will be cut down'. Truly, the hard and mighty are cast down; the soft and weak set on high.

---

1 cf. Chapter 50.
2 The proverb exists in several forms and the text has been tampered with, so that the exact reading is uncertain. But the general sense is quite clear. cf. *Lieh Tzu* II, 16.

Chapter 77

Heaven's way is like the bending of a bow.[1] When a bow is bent the top comes down and the bottom-end comes up. So too does Heaven take away from those who have too much, and give to those that have not enough. But if it is Heaven's way to take from those who have too much and give to those who have not enough, this is far from being man's way. He takes away from those that have not enough in order to make offering to those who already have too much. One there is and one only, so rich that he can afford to make offerings to all under heaven. Who is this? It is the possessor of Tao. If, then, the Sage 'though he controls does not lean, and when he has achieved his aim does not linger',[2] it is because he does not wish to reveal himself as better than others.

1 Not in the act of stringing it but in the act of shooting an arrow from it.
2 over the scene of his triumph. cf. Chapter 2. If he leaned the people would know who it was that was controlling them; if he lingered they would recognise who it was that had .done the work. They would regard him as 'better', 'superior'; and to allow oneself to be so regarded is to sin against 'Heaven's way' and so lose one's power.

Chapter 78

Nothing under heaven is softer or more yielding than
water;[1] but when it attacks things hard and resistant there is
not one of them that can prevail. For they can find no way
of altering[2] it. That the yielding conquers the resistant and
the soft conquers the hard is a fact known by all men, yet
utilised by none. Yet it is in reference to this that the Sage[3]
said 'Only he who has accepted the dirt of the country can
be lord of its soil-shrines;[4] only he who takes upon himself
the evils of the country can become a king among those
that dwell under heaven.' Straight words seem crooked.[5]

1 cf. Chapter 12; also 43.
2 i.e. damaging.
3 Lao Tan. cf. *Chuang Tzu*, XXXIII, 5.
4 Reference to a custom similar to the 'seizin' of medieval Europe,
   whereby a new tenant took a clod of earth in his hand to symbolize
   possession of the soil. The Chinese expression *han hou,* generally used in
   this connection, suggests that the clod was originally held by the new
   feudal lord or tenant between his teeth – a sort of symbolic eating. Thus
   he absorbed the 'virtue' of the soil.
5 seem, as we should say, to be paradoxes.

Chapter 79

To allay the main discontent, but only in a manner that will certainly produce further discontents can hardly be called successful. Therefore the Sage behaves like the holder of the left-hand tally, who stays where he is and does not go round making claims on people. For he who has the 'power' of Tao is the Grand Almoner; he who has not the 'power' is the Grand Perquisitor. 'It is Heaven's way, without distinction of persons, to keep the good perpetually supplied.'[1]

1 see additional notes.

Chapter 80

Given a small country with few inhabitants,[1] he could bring it about that though there should be among the people contrivances requiring ten times, a hundred times less labour,[2] they would not use them. He could bring it about that the people would be ready to lay down their lives and lay them down again[3] in defence of their homes, rather than emigrate. There might still be boats and carriages, but no one would go in them; there might still be weapons of war but no one would drill with them. He could bring it about that 'the people should have no use for any form of writing save knotted ropes,[4] should be contented with their food, pleased with their clothing, satisfied with their homes, should take pleasure in their rustic tasks. The next place might be so near at hand that one could hear the cocks crowing in it, the dogs barking; but the people would grow old and die without ever having been there.'[5]

1 i.e. no need for a large country and many inhabitants which was what the princes of the world pined for.

2 cf. *Shang Tzu* I, 1, and *Chan Kuo Ts'ê* VI, 26, where the principle is laid down that new mechanical contrivances may be accepted if they are ten times more efficient than the old. For the Taoist objection to mechanical contrivances see *Chuang Tzu* XII, 11, already quoted.

3 For *ch'ung-ssu* in the sense of 'die twice over' compare *Lü Shih Ch'un Ch'iu*, 131, end: 'Every one has to die once, but it may be truly said that Ch'ing Fêng died twice over.'

4 One knots ropes as an aid to one's *own* memory (compare our 'tying a knot in one's handkerchief'); whereas one writes contracts down in order to make other people fulfil them. That I think is why 'knotting' belongs to the Golden Age.

5 The passage in inverted commas occurs (with trifling differences) in *Chuang Tzu* (X, 3) as a description of life under the rule of the legendary agricultural Sage Shên-nung. The whole chapter can be understood in the past, present or future tense, as the reader desires.

Chapter 81

True words are not fine-sounding;
Fine-sounding words are not true.
The good man does not prove by argument;
And he who proves by argument[1] is not good.
True wisdom is different from much learning;
Much learning means little wisdom.
The Sage has no need to hoard;
When his own last scrap has been used up on
    behalf of others,
Lo, he has more than before!
When his own last scrap has been used up in
    giving to others,
Lo, he has more than before!
When his own last scrap has been used up in
    giving to others,
Lo, his stock is even greater than before![2]
For Heaven's way is to sharpen without cutting,[3]
And the Sage's way is to act without striving.

---

1 i.e. the 'sophist'.
2 adaptation of a saying that occurs in several forms cf. *Chuang Tzu* XXI, end.
3 to achieve the end without using the material means.

ADDITIONAL NOTES ON TRANSLATION

Chapter 13

For *ching* in the sense 'beside oneself' cf. the story *(Kuo Yü,* 18) of Ho-Lü, famous for his moral zest. On hearing of one good deed this monarch would become so excited that he was *jo ching* 'as it were beside himself'.

In Chinese the word *shên* 'body' also means 'self', and as this word was used to translate the Sanskrit *atman* ('self'). Many Buddhist texts which deal with *atman* ('personality') and not with physical body look in their Chinese dress uncommonly like this passage of the *Tao te ching*. Thus the Chinese version of the Sutra of Dharmapada Parables[1] says: 'Of all evils under heaven none is worse than having a *shên*'. It was natural that the Chinese (and Western writers in their wake) should take *shên* not in its real sense of *atman*, 'self', but as meaning body. Thus Tao-shih[2] in AD 659, commenting on this Dharmapada passage, explains it by quoting *Tao te ching*, Chapter 13, a reference which is in reality quite irrelevant.

Chapter 20

Line 12. Literally 'going up to the Spring Terrace'. This is generally taken merely to mean going up on to a terrace to admire the view. But 'Spring Terrace' balances 'Great Sacrificial-banquet', and must also be the name of a religious ceremony. Now we know from the *Ch'ing Chia Lu*[3] of Ku Lu that 'in the second or third month the richer and more public-spirited among the local gentry pile up a terrace on some open piece of unused ground and provide money for a play. Men and women look on together. It is called the Spring Terrace Play, and is intended to ensure fertility of the crops.' The terrace was of course not intended as a stage, but was a raised bank for the audience to sit on. The fact that men and women, contrary to Chinese custom, sat together indicates that the Spring Terrace was

1 Takakusu, IV, 595a.   2 *Ibidem,* LIV, p. 63.
3 I know this book only in quotation.

originally the scene of a kind of carnival, a period of authorized license intended, as such festivals always are, to promote the fertility of the fields. It is of course a far cry from the eighteenth century (Ku Lu's period) to the third century BC; but I think it may in any case be taken as certain that some kind of carnival is referred to.

Chapter 21

A 'charge' (*ming*) consists of the 'life-giving words' that a general addresses to troops before a battle or the instructions that a king gives to a new feudal lord or minister. The object of this charge is to 'animate' the troops, lord, or minister, with a particular purpose. For this reason he speaks 'words of good cheer', which is the root meaning of the character I have translated 'cheers onward'. The 'ten thousand things' are compared to troops in whose ears the general's (i.e. Tao's) orders of the day still ring.

Chapter 31

'In peace the left-hand side is the place of honour . . . ' We know too that circumambulatory rites were in civil life performed clockwise; but in war, anti-clockwise. The distinction is a very important one in all primitive ritual, cf. *I Chou Shu* 32. 'It is the way of Heaven to prefer the right; the sun and moon travel westward. It is the way of earth to prefer the left; the watercourses flow to the east . . . In rites of good omen, circumambulation is to the left; it follows the way of earth, in order that the performers themselves may be benefited. In ceremonies of war, circumambulation is to the right; it follows the way of Heaven, in order that the weapons may gain in sharpness.'

Chapter 38

The *tao* (doctrine) of which foreknowledge was the flower is of course not Taoism, but may well be the branch of Confucianism represented, for example, by the *Doctrine of the Mean* (paragraph 24): 'The way of complete fulfilment (of one's own nature) leads to knowledge of what is to come.' Support for the idea of the Sage as prophet was found in *Analects* II, 23.[4] See also *Lu Shih Ch'un Ch'iu*, P'ien 85, where a whole section is devoted to foreknowledge. The

4 'Can ten generations hence be foreknown?'

Dualists and systematizers of theories based on the Five Elements also
went in for prophecy. It is unlikely that diviners by the *Book of
Changes* are meant, for this work is seldom alluded to by writers of the
third century and did not become part of the Confucian curriculum
till the Han dynasty. As the clauses which go before are directed
against Confucianism, it seems likely that it is a Confucian doctrine
that is here condemned.

Chapter 46

Chiao means here not the 'outskirts' of the kingdom, but the mound
on the outskirts of the capital, scene of the Great Sacrifice which
inaugurated the season's agriculture. To let weeds grow on this
mound was a sacrilege,[5] and to breed war-horses upon it, a double
profanation. For the Great Sacrifice is essentially connected with
peace.

'Lure.' The root means 'fluttering' like a bird. Hence (1) to set a
trap, to lure. (2) to be caught in meshes (of the law), a criminal. (3)
that which involves one in such meshes, a crime.

Chapter 53

Chieh-jan, 'the least scrap of'. cf. *Lieh Tzu* IV, 2, 'The least scrap of
any existing thing, the least whisper of sound . . . ' It can also be used
of time: 'A hill-way used only for the least little while turns into a
well-defined path . . . (*Mencius* VII, II, 21).

Chapter 79

It was believed[6] that in the time of the ancient Sages a certain
proportion of land in each village had been set aside as 'common
land' and its produce handed over to officials to be used for
communal purposes, such as (1) the support of the aged and needy,
(2) the support of officials. Under the Yin dynasty, it was said, this
system was known as 'labour-loaning', because the villagers lent their
labour to the community. This term came to have the meaning

---

5 compare *Hzun Tzu*, P'ien 16, end: 'He who does not sweep the
   droppings at home is not likely to notice that weeds run riot on the *chiao*
   mound'.
6 what relation these beliefs bear to any actual, ancient system of tithe it is
   hard to say.

'assistance', because the needy were 'helped' out of the fund so established. But it also came to mean 'taxation', because the produce was handed over to and in part used by officials. The author here uses the term assistance ('Almoner', literally 'Assister') in the first sense. In the Chou dynasty, it was said, various local systems of tithe were replaced by a 'general' system, and the word 'general' *(ch'ê)* came to mean tithing, tax-exaction. This is the word here used in the phrase *ssu-ch'ê* ,'controller of taxes, perquisitor'.

Tallies played in the life of the early Chinese the same part that tickets, cheques, etc., do in Europe today. They were used as 'passes' of admission to fortified places, as 'tickets' entitling the owners to a share in sacrificial meat, as 'cheques' in commerce. The importance of the tally in actual life is attested by the great variety of metaphorical senses in which the expression 'fitting the tallies' is used by early writers. Thus Mencius (IV, 2, 1) says that the methods of all the Sages, both former and latter, 'fit like tallies'. The Codifiers said that if everything helpful and everything inimical to the State were defined, the ruler would merely have to 'fit the tallies' by allotting rewards and punishments according to the Code. It is used of deeds that are 'as good as' words, of theories that work in practice, and finally at a later date, of the successful 'fitting together' of ingredients in alchemy.

WORDSWORTH CLASSICS
OF WORLD LITERATURE

APULEIUS
The Golden Ass

ARISTOTLE
The Nicomachean Ethics

MARCUS AURELIUS
Meditations

FRANCIS BACON
The Essays of Sir Francis Bacon

JOHN BUNYAN
The Pilgrim's Progress

KARL VON CLAUSEWITZ
On War (abridged)

CONFUCIUS
The Analects

CHARLES DARWIN
Voyage of the Beagle

DESCARTES
*Key Philosophical
Writings*

SIGMUND FREUD
The Interpretation of Dreams

EDWARD GIBBON
*The Decline and Fall of the
Roman Empire (abridged)*

KHALIL GIBRAN
The Prophet

HERODOTUS
Histories

HORACE
Selected Odes

LAO TZU
Tao te ching

T. E. LAWRENCE
Seven Pillars of Wisdom

SIR THOMAS MALORY
Le Morte Darthur

JOHN STUART MILL
*On Liberty & The Subjection
of Women*

SIR THOMAS MORE
Utopia

THOMAS PAINE
Rights of Man

MARCO POLO
The Travels

SAMUEL PEPYS
Selections from the Diary

PLATO
*The Symposium &
the Death of Socrates*

The Republic

LA ROCHEFOUCAULD
Maxims

JEAN-JACQUES ROUSSEAU
The Confessions

SUETONIUS
Lives of the Twelve Caesars

THUCYDIDES
*The History of the
Peloponnesian War*